ADVANCE PRAISE FOR
Our Changing World

"*Our Changing World* is an astounding, profound and practical analysis and set of guidelines for emerging from the COVID-19 pandemic into the new reality of post-pandemic times. Most importantly it suggests that life in the new time can be one with room for all people. Readers learn how to shed what keeps us from healing and living in loving interrelationships with others and our home, the earth. Sally Severino's ability to extract just what humankind needs to know and do to live in concert with all creation is simply, beautifully and meaningfully presented, leading readers through global crisis to an emerging paradigm of justice and love." —**Betsy Diaz, Ph.D./Counseling Psychology, Pre-school and Elementary School Teacher**

"Dealing with change has always been an important skill in life, though frequently disregarded. In recent years, this skill is becoming even more important. Dr. Severino helps with this process by personal examples, discussion of the literature, and directed meditations and exercises, which allow an exploration of a new paradigm for seeing and healing ourselves and our world. *Our Changing World* is incredibly prophetic, identifying clearly a catalyst for change amidst the turmoil of a pandemic and the social unrest of the year 2020."
—**Daniel F. Housholder, MD, FACR (Ret.)**

"What I have always appreciated most about Sally Severino is her honest, reality-based, hopeful, all-embracing view of life. She finds the spiritual meaning in everything, no matter how distressing or discouraging—even the election of Donald Trump. As she puts it, Trump 'mirrors for us the destructive aspects of our collective unconscious. . . . While it may not be his intention, his behavior is shouting to us, 'Stop doing what I'm doing!' I cannot think of a more helpful lens through which to view our troubling times." —**Paula Huston's most recent book is *One Ordinary Sunday: A Meditation on the Mystery of the Mass*.**

"This latest contribution by Sally Severino, MD, will be a huge help to those who take the time to read it thoughtfully, do the exercises reflectively and honestly, and then take the insights gained into the rest of their lives as tools to continue their personal and communal journey into oneness consciousness. I know that I will be reading it again and again gaining something with each reading that I was not ready to receive the first time. Additionally, the author quotes from many reliable sources should the reader desire to pursue any or all of them for deeper and clearer understanding. Pure deliciousness!!" **—Sister Ann Marie Klasky, CSSF**

"In today's global society, where everything is politicized and spun as an either-or choice pitting people against each other, *Our Changing World* brings a fresh perspective that in reality the universe has put us on a great collision course for unity." —**Sid McGregor, Corrective Lens Podcast – sidmcgregor.com**

"Psychiatrist and psychoanalyst Sally Severino offers an engaging and moving account of her journey towards personal wholeness through our recent national stresses and a series of personal losses. A long-time advocate of contemplative prayer, in this book she explains how oneness with God becomes real when suffering forces our identity to expand from 'me' to 'us,' and then to all of creation. It is through this process that we find our true selves and our greatest fulfillment." —**Ian Osborn, MD, Author of** *Tormenting Thoughts and Secret Rituals: The Hidden Epidemic of Obsessive-Compulsive Disorder* **and** *Can Christianity Cure Obsessive Compulsive Disorder? A Psychiatrist Explores the Role of Faith in Treatment*

ALSO BY SALLY K. SEVERINO, MD

Sacred Desire: Growing in Compassionate Living

Becoming Fire: A Freudian Psychoanalyst's Spiritual Journey

Behold Our Moral Body: Psychiatry, Duns Scotus and Neuroscience

Felician Franciscan Sisters in the Southwest: A History of the Felician Sisters of the Assumption of the Blessed Virgin Mary Province (1963-2009)

Wellness in Mind: Your Brain's Surprising Secrets to Gaining Health from the Inside Out

Being Image: Simple Exercises to Claiming Your Authentic Being

Our Changing World

UNDERSTANDING AND COPING WITH IT

Sally K. Severino, MD

EPIGRAPH BOOKS

RHINEBECK, NEW YORK

Our Changing World: Understanding and Coping with It © 2020 by Sally K. Severino, MD

All rights reserved. No part of this work may be used or reproduced in any manner without written permission from the author except in critical articles or reviews. Contact the publisher for information.

Paperback ISBN 978-1-951937-50-8
eBook ISBN 978-1-951937-51-5

Library of Congress Control Number 2020912352

Book and cover design by Colin Rolfe
Cover image by Morning Brew

Epigraph Books
22 East Market Street, Suite 304
Rhinebeck, NY 12572
(845) 876-486
epigraphps.com

DEDICATION

For Evelyn M. Miller in gratitude for the decades
you modeled for me how to live with integrity and zest.

Contents

Author's Note xi
Introduction xiii

Part I
FORCES TOWARD A NEW WORLD PARADIGM

Chapter 1	Presidential Election 2016	3
Chapter 2	Facing Death and Enduring Suffering	9
Chapter 3	COVID-19 Pandemic 2020	18

Part II
NEW IMAGE OF A HUMAN BEING

Chapter 4	The First Half of Life: Establishing an Identity of "Me"	29
Chapter 5	The Second Half of Life: Establishing an Identity of "Us"	35
Chapter 6	Getting to I AM	42

Part III
LIVING IN COMMUNION

Chapter 7	The Transcendent Self	51
Chapter 8	Oneness Consciousness	57
Chapter 9	Hope in Times of Turmoil	65

Postscript: Racial Unrest 2020 73
Acknowledgements 79
References 81

Author's Note

The story in Chapter 2 entitled "Sally's Journey to a New Way of Seeing" first appeared in the book *Being Image: Simple Exercises to Claim Your Authentic Being* written by Andrew Garrison, MS CPT CHC and Sally K. Severino, MD. Raleigh, NC: Lulu Press, Inc., 2019.

Introduction

Our world is changing, in some frightening and challenging ways. It seems clear that, if we are to survive as a species, we are each being called upon to create a new image of what it means to be human, and how to live with other humans in communion.

Here's a true story to give you an idea of what "living in communion" with others means.

One weekend, while my friend Pat and her husband were lunching at their favorite casino, a couple approached them. The man asked Pat's husband where he got his walker, saying he needed one after his back surgery. After they told him, the man thanked them, admired the crucifix Pat's husband was wearing, and, turning to his wife, pointed to Pat's red cross with silver trim and said, "Look, how beautiful!"

The man's wife exclaimed, "Yes, it is!" and her eyes met Pat's for a moment.

Spontaneously, Pat asked her, "Are you Catholic?" In unison, the couple replied, "Yes."

Without hesitating, Pat removed the cross from her neck and handed it to the woman with a gesture to put it on.

"Oh no," the woman said, "I can't possibly accept it."

"Yes, you can," Pat encouraged. "I want you to have it."

The woman thanked Pat and the couple went their own way.

An hour or so later, the two couples met again. This time they exchanged names and Pat said to the woman, "I hope you'll wear the crucifix."

She answered, "I will wear it every day. You have no idea how special this gift is to me. Today is the birthday of my son, who died. I feel that receiving this cross has been a gift from God."

Why start with this particular story? Because it gives an example of the kind of people our changing world urges us to be: people who give freely in love to each other. When Pat gave the woman her cross and the woman shared her gratitude, they freely gave love to each other. Such acts of freely loving and sharing create relationships in communion, and help to create a more cooperative, loving, and caring world.

Our Changing World is a three-part approach that will help transform both yourself and your relationships with others. Part I (Forces toward a New World Paradigm) is my personal story. Asking questions of my experience of pain and suffering turned that experience into a doorway, and stimulated my curiosity just as it will yours. Part II (New Image of a Human Being) invites you to explore the science of being human, laying the foundation for changing our image of who we think we are. And in Part III (Living in Communion) you will discover the exciting possibilities for a world inhabited by people who have done the self-transformation work.

As you hone your connectivity skills, with the help of meditations and exercises designed to encourage you, you will learn how to claim your transcendent self and move toward oneness consciousness. And it is good to know that, while each of us is an authentic one-of-a-kind person unfolding in relationship with all creation, because we are all interconnected, we can relate to the process of each other's unfolding and rejoice in each other's triumphs.

Before continuing, I feel the need to make a big disclaimer. In this book I have conceptualized and written about personhood and being as though they can be known by our mind. In fact, our only knowledge of them *is* our mind. Oneness consciousness is based in the seamless intimacy of experiencing. However, the majority of us – including me – have not realized oneness consciousness. Hopefully, this book will help all of us move toward that goal. For those who live in oneness consciousness, I apologize for what is not in fact absolutely true of your experience.

Part I — Forces Toward a New World Paradigm

Chapter 1 – PRESIDENTIAL ELECTION 2016. The election of Donald Trump to the Presidency of the United States dumbfounded many around the world, and frightened me into searching for meaning in the event. The answers I found can show you the nature of our greatest challenge: to take responsibility for what we decide is truth.

Chapter 2 – FACING DEATH AND ENDURING SUFFERING. When I experienced sudden onset small bowel obstruction, I learned some important lessons from enduring pain and facing my own death: I realized that we must learn to see in a new and different way. The chapter includes a questionnaire exercise that can jumpstart your own journey to a change of consciousness.

Chapter 3 – COVID-19 PANDEMIC 2020. The global pandemic may well have been a turning point. What does a pandemic encourage in human beings? Perhaps it is an opportunity to experience global solidarity, to explore the characteristics of a WeWorld instead of a MeWorld. Here we will examine the difference between I-I relationships versus I-It and I-Thou relationships, along with an exercise to help you open to the new paradigm of co-creating together.

Part II — New Image of a Human Being

Chapter 4 – THE FIRST HALF OF LIFE: ESTABLISHING AN IDENTITY OF "ME". The first half of life teaches us that we are different from all others. How we are equipped to learn who "me" is, is explained neurologically, psychologically and biologically. To gain a firm sense of "me" is important because it enables us to read, calculate and think objectively and critically.

Chapter 5 – THE SECOND HALF OF LIFE: ESTABLISHING AN IDENTITY OF "US". Because an identity of "me" is incomplete, the second half of life calls us to grow into the fullness of our deeper nature, an identity of "us." Here you will find neurological, psychological, and biological explanations of the ways we are equipped to do this. An identity of "us" allows us to see the world with a perception of oneness. Included are two exercises to help you begin seeing with oneness consciousness.

Chapter 6 – GETTING TO I AM. To know I AM is to be in touch with one's central core energy. Energy is activity. I AM is activity. I AM is a conduit for the flow of energy. Read about the four characteristics of I AM, along with a story that describes one person's experience. Then you can try the exercise to begin changing your perception of yourself.

Part III — Living in Communion

Chapter 7 – THE TRANSCENDENT SELF. Transcendent self is another name for I AM. We experience it when we let go all the descriptions of ourselves that we learned in the first half of life and connect with our core loving energy. Here you will learn the four steps for connecting with your transcendent self, the self that connects us with the energy that began our universe, and launches us into living with creative freedom.

Chapter 8 – ONENESS CONSCIOUSNESS. Oneness consciousness is a consciousness of whole persons, persons who have found their I AM and embraced their transcendent selves. Here you will discover how personhood is defined and functions within oneness consciousness, as well as how living in oneness consciousness readies us for a massive world transformation.

Chapter 9 – HOPE IN TIMES OF TURMOIL. How do we willingly participate in the larger mystery of life? We begin by accepting what is happening. The very meaning of being alive is to be continually in the process of becoming a new creation. Unbinding ourselves and others from the turmoil life invariably brings frees us to welcome life as it evolves.

May this view of our changing world offer you encouragement and hope as you change and transform to meet life's challenges.

Part I

Forces Toward a New World Paradigm

My convictions about our changing world were stirred by three events:

- the election of Donald Trump to the presidency of the United States in 2016,
- facing death and enduring suffering in 2019,
- and the COVID-19 Pandemic in 2020.

    This section describes these three events.

Chapter I

Presidential Election 2016

> ... *if we think of the evolution of a man as the inner connecting up with an already existing possibility—just as an oak-tree is a possibility in an acorn, being a higher level of an acorn—and that this connecting up can only be possible through a growing intensity of insight*...
>
> **Maurice Nicoll**
> *The New Man*

These are worrisome and frightening times. When Donald Trump was elected president of the United States in 2016, I became acutely focused on trying to understand what was happening in the world. In my search, I discovered two books, one written by Cynthia Bourgeault, an Episcopal priest (2013), and the other written by Richard Rohr, O.F.M. who is a Catholic priest (2016). Both books gave me hopeful insights as to what might be occurring in our nation and the world. In particular, it gave me one way to understand the forces leading up to Donald Trump's election and his role in what is occurring in our nation and around the globe.

Many believe that there is a worldwide movement toward a new paradigm, one that embraces the interconnected oneness of the universe. Both Bourgeault and Rohr claim that in the process of evolving change, there is an ancient principle undergirding all new creations. This ancient principle is known as the *Law of Three*. This law, rearticulated in the early twentieth century by the Armenian-born teacher, G. I. Gurdjief (1866-1949), says that in every new creation there are three forces involved: (1) a force that pushes toward change, (2) a force that pushes against change, and (3) a force that provides an opportunity to address what is preventing change. The three forces are morally neutral and indispensable. Their interweaving produces a fourth—a new creation—in a new dimension.

When we apply this rule to the current movement toward interconnection, and to Donald Trump's role in it, it seems clear that: (1) the force pushing us toward interconnected oneness is seen in ecology where a change in one environment affects all environments, and in economics and communications where we are becoming a single global network; (2) the force pushing against this change is manifest in the poor getting poorer while the rich are getting richer and in global warming where nature protests against our human dominion; (3) the third force is Donald Trump who mirrors for us the destructive aspects of our collective unconscious. He name-calls, shouts and threatens war; he spews forth upset and anger when we react to this or that; he touts being right and morally superior. Psychologically he is doing his job to provoke consciousness-raising and consciousness reflection, debate, and dialogue. While it may not be his intention, his behavior is shouting to us, "Look, people! I am showing you the behaviors that bring planetary destruction. Wake up! Take responsibility! Stop doing what I'm doing!"

When we can recognize the destructive forces of our collective unconscious and own them, those forces are weakened and there is hope for a new consciousness of oneness to be birthed.

Where Do We Start?

One place to begin is by taking responsibility for what we decide is truth. Realize that simply saying something is factual (or an "alternative fact") doesn't make it true. In fact, "facts" can hide truth and be used to serve any agenda.

Timothy Snyder, Levin Professor of History at Yale University, claims that truth dies in four ways (2017, 66-68):

> **1. When there is open hostility to verifiable reality.**
> He states that President Trump does this frequently and gives as an example the following: "One attempt during the 2016 Campaign to track his utterances found that 78 percent of his factual claims were false" (66).
>
> **2. When there are repeated incantations designed to make the fictional plausible.**
> He writes, "The systematic use of nicknames such as 'Lyin' Ted' and 'Crooked Hillary' displaced certain character traits that might more appropriately have been affixed to the president himself. Yet through blunt repetition over Twitter, our president managed the transformation of individuals into stereotypes that people then spoke aloud" (67).
>
> **3. When there is open embrace of contradiction.**
> "The president's campaign involved the promises of cutting taxes for everyone, eliminating the national debt, and

increasing spending on both social policy and national defense. These promises mutually contradict" (67).

4. When there is misplaced faith.
"It involves the sort of self-deifying claims the president made when he said that 'I alone can solve it' or 'I am your voice'" (68).

I use these examples not to vilify President Trump, but to underscore what he is showing us. If President Trump's role in our evolving world is to provoke reflection, debate and dialogue, then let us reflect, debate, and dialogue. This is why his election stirred me to wonder what is going on in the world and brought me to the realization that we each need to take responsibility for becoming more aware of what is true.

Our perspective is important when deciding what is true. Is our perspective one of relative or of absolute truth? "As an illustration of relative and absolute truth, consider the sunrise and sunset. When we say the sun rises in the morning and sets in the evening, that is truth, but only relatively. In absolute terms, it is false. Only from the limited perspective of an observer on or near the planet's surface does the sun rise and set. If you were far out in space, you would see that the sun neither rises nor sets, but that it shines continuously" (Tolle 2005/2016, 281). It is absolute truth that we hope to become more aware of and to live from.

What does it mean to start living from truth? Judy Cannato, Certified Mid-Life Directions Consultant, writes that when we begin living from truth, we realize that it is love we most deeply desire. "Love that connects our lives, love that binds our brokenness, love that heals divisions, love that forgives and turns us in a new direction—love is the heart of [our] vision" (2003, 10). But we must choose to trust in the power of love to connect us with each other and transform us individually and co-creatively. And, we must hope that President Trump keeps doing what he is doing until we become so aware of reality that we tip our world into a new creation of oneness consciousness.

Later on, we will explore more fully what oneness consciousness is. But for now, try these practices that will help to make you more deeply aware of reality.

Focusing Practices

All exercises in this book are intended to complement rather than replace physical and mental medical evaluations and treatments.

1 - Sit quietly and notice each physical sensation in your body. Consciously let go of each physical sensation as you notice it. Do this one moment at a time.

2 - When you begin to simply feel and exist, with no agenda, no willful manipulation, you begin to experience the inner bliss of nothingness. While this is a difficult state to achieve—some people spend decades meditating and pursuing spiritual practices to get there—when you do feel moments of total nothingness, you find closer connection with your true Being. So make it a habit to simply BE for a few minutes every day.

3 - Create time to be in nature. Give yourself time to savor the sounds or the silence.

Look, don't interpret. See the light, colors, shapes.

Listen, don't judge the sounds.

Touch something and feel its Being.

Open to the reality of what is. Observe the rhythm of your breathing. Feel the air flowing in and out. Feel the life energy inside your body.

4 - Give away something you don't use at least once every day. Enjoy the process of emptying, and of feeling that what you release may have value to someone else.

Chapter 2

Facing Death and Enduring Suffering

Real suffering belongs to innocence, not guilt.

Helen Luke
The Way of Woman

The morning of October 1, 2019, I awoke with severe abdominal pain and nausea. Urgent Care sent me directly to Rust Hospital Emergency to rule out intestinal obstruction, a condition common in women with a history of abdominal surgery. In my case, I had undergone surgery to remove a dermoid cyst from my right ovary when I was in my thirties. I was now eighty-two.

Treatment began with resting my gut—meaning I wasn't allowed to eat anything—that would hopefully restore function without surgery. A naso-gastric (N/G) tube was inserted through my nose into my stomach to keep the nausea under control and prevent vomiting. This was not only uncomfortable, but painfully irritating to my nose and throat. In addition, the medicines they gave me intravenously ruined every vein they put an IV in, so I had to have multiple IVs and I was black, blue, and purple from wrists to elbows on both arms.

On October 4th, things seemed to be moving forward so they took out the N/G tube. After a lunch of clear fluids, they gave me an oral medicine, but because my esophagus was irritated from the N/G tube, the pill stuck at the irritation point. All the fluids I took to dislodge it immobilized my gut again.

By now I was wondering if I would survive this ordeal. I asked to see a priest and Father JP from St. Michael and All Angels Episcopal Church gave me final rites.

On October 7th, the N/G tube was reinserted and laparoscopic surgery was performed that showed adhesions in my small bowel. These were cut to allow my bowel to reopen. By October 8th, my bowels resumed their grumblings, the N/G tube was pulled, and I was put on a clear fluid diet.

In all, I had been fasting for seven days. I was exhausted, bruised, puffy from 16 pounds of fluids that had infiltrated my tissues, and suffering pain every time I swallowed, a leftover from the N/G tube irritation.

I was discharged from the hospital October 11th with instructions not to rush back to Planet Fitness and OsteoStrong, due to the danger of causing a hernia. It was January 2020 before I regained enough energy to resume physical workouts.

What I Learned from Suffering

For seven days I endured suffering: both the physical suffering of hunger and pain and the psychospiritual suffering of facing possible death. I learned that suffering is not lethal; indeed it seemed to play an essential role in my growing awareness of who I truly am. More accurately, perhaps, suffering taught me that I was different from—and more than—all the labels I attributed to myself early in life when I established my identity of "intelligent, capable of taking care of myself, and successful."

Feeling vulnerable and weak, I spent much of those long hospital days and nights in meditation and prayer, readying myself to surrender to whatever was to be. I knew I had control over nothing except whether to fight or to surrender. I had always thought of myself as a fighter. Surrendering was a different way of being, a way of being in relationship with the will of the universe. This was not a relationship between two entities. This was a new and different kind of my Being in relationship. The universe and I were co-creative partners. I came to know in a new and very deep way that the universe was part of me and I was part of the universe.

Perhaps some of you are familiar with the Enneagram, an ancient system for understanding yourself and others, which describes nine basic personality types. I am an Enneagram eight personality. An eight is a gut person whose basic fear is not being in control, of being destroyed. I experienced this health crisis as hitting me where I am most vulnerable—my gut. As I surrendered all the old definitions of myself from the first half of my life, and accepted myself as being someone different, I discovered that I could be compassionate with everyone who helped to take care of me. Out of surrender, flowed love.

After my recovery, I happened upon a book by Donald Kalshed, a Jungian analyst, entitled *Trauma and the Soul* (2013). Kalshed identified two kinds of suffering: suffering with bitter resentment, and suffering with willing acceptance. His account of suffering with willing acceptance seemed to be what I called surrender to whatever was going to be. No matter what I called it, my suffering left me at peace with all that was happening to me.

Not only was the hospitalization an experience of suffering with willing acceptance, but it was strikingly linked to a previous experience: I was hospitalized *exactly* two years to the day from the date that my housemate of twenty-some years was hospitalized with a broken hip. That story was told in a book I co-authored with Andrew Garrison (2019), but it deserves to be retold here because its lessons are relevant to this book and to my continuing understanding of what is occurring in our world at this time.

My Journey to a New Quality of Seeing

It all began on Sunday, October 1st. When I looked out the back door, I saw my housemate, Evelyn, lying face down on our patio. "What are you doing?" I asked. "I fell," Evelyn said through gritted teeth. "Help me get up. I don't think I broke anything because I can move." Together we managed to get her into a patio chair. "Call our neighbors." Evelyn said. "Find out if they still have a walker; I'll need one to get into the house." My frantic telephone calls led nowhere. Finally, I told Evelyn that I was calling 911.

"We'll be right there," the EMT told me. "Do not try to move her! Secure any animals." I hastily shut Evelyn's Chihuahua, Chusca, in her bedroom. Because of Evelyn's pain, it took four burly men to get her into the ambulance. "On a scale of 1 to 10, how much pain are you in?" asked one. "7.5," answered Evelyn. "We'll rate you 10 on cooperation," replied the man.

After letting Chusca out of her enclosure, I headed to Hospital Emergency where we found out that Evelyn had a hip fracture. She underwent total hip replacement the next day. In the ensuing week I rushed between hospital and home, tending to Evelyn's needs, Chusca's needs, and the needs of our house. Thanks be for good neighbors!! One offered to mow our lawn weekly when he mowed his, and another volunteered to walk Chusca and to keep a key to our house along with instructions for Chusca's care, in case anything should happen to me in the midst of all the stress I was experiencing. I also scheduled to have my shower head converted to a hand-held model so that Evelyn could use my shower upon returning home. She would never again be able to sit down and bathe in her bathtub.

At the hospital, Evelyn was learning how to use instruments to help her dress, and she was learning how to walk again. At home I arranged for Chusca to be bathed and have her nails clipped at PetSmart. That appointment was scheduled for Monday morning, October 9. While Chusca was being bathed, I rushed to Kmart for an elevated toilet seat for Evelyn's toilet and a plastic chair for my shower so that Evelyn could sit on it. All of this was to occur after Evelyn went from the hospital to Rehab. What none of us anticipated was the fact that Monday was Columbus Day, a national holiday. This meant that Evelyn's application to Rehab never received financial approval because the offices were closed. Since her hospital length of stay had maxed out, she was discharged home that very day.

Between neighbors and workmen that I hired, my shower head got converted to a hand held model and the shower chair and toilet seat got assembled by the time I arrived home from the hospital with Evelyn. Three weeks of hell then ensued.

Evelyn needed my help to get to her toilet every two or three hours throughout the night. I began sleeping on our living room couch because I could not hear her call me when I slept in my bedroom. Within five days she developed diarrhea. Diapers could not contain the mess. I made frantic trips to Walgreens for more diapers and bed pads.

Fortunately, we had a follow-up appointment with the assistant to her orthopedic surgeon the following Tuesday. Since I was too tired to drive her safely, a neighbor drove both of us. The physician assistant who saw us seemed unconcerned about the diarrhea and assured us that the surgical site was healing well. The next day we had a post-hospital checkup with the physician covering for Evelyn's PCP. He ordered cholestyramine and Lomotil for the diarrhea, neither of which helped at all. By Friday midday, I insisted we go to the hospital emergency room. There they obtained stool and blood samples. Evelyn was dehydrated and hypokalemic. We were discharged home with a prescription for potassium chloride and probiotics to await the results of the stool culture. Sunday we received the diagnosis: C-diff colitis. Evelyn began an eight-day course of Flagyl and I began wearing rubber gloves and cleaning everything with Lysol. I had been careful cleaning up Evelyn's diarrhea, but not careful enough for C-diff. Would I come down with the bug?

By the last day of the antibiotic, we were both exhausted and hopeless. Evelyn had me call her priest for a home visit, send Chusca back to Chihuahua rescue, and apply for her long-term care to cover assisted living or hospice.

The next morning life turned around. Our downhill course into depression and despair turned uphill. Evelyn's diarrhea stopped. Her priest gave her hope. We called Chihuahua rescue to bring Chusca back. Once the uphill course began, it never stopped.

But I had been changed during the downhill plunge. The process had so exhausted me that I was too tired to think. All I could do was live in each moment; my entire life became a present moment meditation. In each present moment I sensed and felt the communion between Evelyn and me and those supporting us. My eyes saw only the reality of the love that flowed through the process. It manifested itself in a certain synchrony. Despite all the procedural glitches, recovery setbacks, and less-than-optimal flow of care, there was a miraculous timing that I experienced. Help would come at just the right time or I would be in just the right place at the right time to do what was needed. I wondered: perhaps synchronicity is not a rare occurrence after all. Perhaps it's the organizing principle of energy but we are oblivious to it most of the time.

Living in the flow of love allowed me a glimpse of my true Being. How? I'm not totally sure. For one thing, I experienced gratitude, humor, and wonder right in the midst of all the shit (quite literally). And I do believe that I learned a little about surrender and servanthood—perhaps not permanently, but I experienced them as I never had before. I neither fought the situation nor myself. I found I was able to act out of care for the welfare of others. And, I faced death in a more accepting way.

This was my real Being as I had never felt it before. I felt it in the raw experience of my human identity, in the present moment seeing with my heart, rather than in the past and future of seeing with my head. This was what Michael Brown calls heart knowing or "vibrational awareness" (2010, 41). We are experiencing what we already are yet haven't remembered. For me this meant that in the midst of all the sorrow and suffering, I experienced overwhelming gratitude that I had been given this work to do. I had never before in my life experienced myself as a good servant. I felt I was one with Evelyn. We were in this together no matter what the outcome.

The experience of oneness reminded me of the words of the renowned Jungian analyst, Helen M. Luke, "The experience of this kinship, this unity, has been described by great poets, artists, and mystics of all ages; and in our own century have been added the voices not only of the psychologists but finally of the quantum physicists themselves, exploring the subatomic world. The reality of all life is an unceasing dance on all levels of being, material, instinctual, psychic, and spiritual, in which every motion of the tiniest part, weaving patterns of exchange and transformation, affects the whole. … since the dawn of consciousness, it seems that there is a mystery at the center of all these movements of the dance which has, in the dimension of linear time, always pressed up from below, down from above, to awaken in individual human beings a growing awareness of *meaning*. Then a recognition of the patterns of the dance becomes possible in our own lives, an intuition of the interdependence of each with all which is at the same time the gateway to freedom of spirit and the sunrise of eternity" (1987/2010, 60-61).

The experience of oneness requires a change of consciousness: a change from efficiency to love, empathy, and participation; a change from competition to cooperation; and a change from technology to ecology (Garrison & Severino 2019, 50-53).

Asking yourself a few questions can start you on the path toward your own change of consciousness. Here is a questionnaire exercise for you to try.

Questionnaire Exercise

This exercise is adapted from Michael Dowd's book *Thank God for Evolution: How the Marriage of Science and Religion will Transform Your Life and Our World*. New York: PLUME: Penguin Group, 2007/2009, 59-60.

To live your unique Being with integrity means "getting right with Reality ... by growing in humility, authenticity, responsibility, and service to the Whole" (Dowd 2007/2009, 59). So, ask yourself these four questions. While I give answers that may resonate with you, you may also want to respond in your own words.

Why humility? Because humility puts you in touch with Reality. You are not the center of the Universe; you were born out of it. You need the Universe and the Universe needs you.

Why authenticity? Because authenticity aligns you with Reality so that human beings and all creation can grow together in healthy ways.

Why responsibility? "Because what's really *real* is that there is only one person responsible for the quality of your life, and that person is you" (Dowd 2007/2009, 60).

Why service to the Whole? Because it is our source and sustenance. We are part of the Universe; we are all growing and developing together.

Chapter 3

COVID-19 Pandemic 2020

> *... knowledge should always lead to understanding and that understanding is only possible with a corresponding development of being.*
>
> **Maurice Nicoll**
> *The New Man*

The United States presidential election of 2016 and my personal health crisis of 2019 scared me enough! Then, the COVID-19 Pandemic hit. It roared into New Mexico, where I was living, in March 2020. Suddenly life changed. The pandemic radically transformed stock markets and the very nature of life, with millions out of work, streets and shops empty and healthcare systems under strain. What's scarier than the Coronavirus?

Suddenly I saw people *reacting* with fear, thinking only of themselves, hoarding food and toilet paper. I also saw those *responding* with suffering and feeling that we were all in this together; we're all subject to this crisis. The pandemic shook our global world and our very being.

In Chapter 1, I described a view that I agree with: that Donald

Trump's election to presidency reflects a movement occurring worldwide towards a new paradigm that embraces the interconnected oneness of the universe. In Chapter 2, I described personal experiences that taught me at least two lessons: (1) great suffering can lead to great love and (2) suffering can teach us that we are all one.

It is no surprise, then, that I see the pandemic as an opportunity to experience global solidarity. Globally, when a pandemic hits, we are all in the crisis together.

WeWorld not just a MeWorld

Anthropologist Thomas de Zengotita coined the word MeWorld (de Zengotita 2005/2007). I suggest that the COVID-19 Pandemic is urging us to see and endorse that we live in a WeWorld not just a MeWorld. What do I mean by that?

As I define it, the MeWorld that we live in has understood human relationships to be either I-It relationships or I-Thou relationships. I am using these relationship descriptions in the same manner that author Beatrice Bruteau (2001) uses them. In I-It relationships, we as a subject relate to another as an object. In I-Thou relationships, we as a subject respond to another in dialogue. Both of these relationships are face-to-face relationships.

The WeWorld calls for I-I relationships (Bruteau 2001) where two subjects—each facing the same direction—enter into each other's experience and know each other's experience simultaneously: each subject knows from their combined experiencing together, like two streams flowing together to form one river. There is both difference and union: two streams and one river. The I-I relationship is a new way of being as Maurice Nicoll suggests in the epigraph to this chapter.

Each of the relationships, I-It, I-Thou and I-I, maintains separate individuals while simultaneously establishing themselves as persons in union—but not in the same way. In I-It and I-Thou relationships, difference is established as subject to object. In I-I relationships, difference is established as subject to subject. In I-It and I-Thou relationships, unity is imposed from without and is extrinsic to the persons being unified. In I-I relationships, unity comes from within the persons being united and must be freely accepted.

MeWorld	**WeWorld**
Human Relationships:	Human Relationships:
I-It and I-Thou	I-I
Domination	Enhancement
Non-reciprocal being	Reciprocal being
Unity:	Unity:
Achieved by being imposed from without	Is from inside and must be freely chosen
Self-identity:	Self-identity:
Uses negation and separation to set external boundaries	Attained by mutual affirmation and giving ones' selves to enhance one another

I believe the COVID-19 Pandemic is urging us toward living in I-I relationships. But to accomplish this, we need to change the typical way we see and understand everything.

Before we explore a different way of seeing and understanding, though, we need to do what we can to alleviate the stress of being quarantined at home. The following helpful tips, first written by

Margie Donian, a New York City psychologist, can be adapted to any time of difficulty in our lives. Here is my summary of her tips:

Mental Health Tips for Quarantine

1. Stick to a routine.
Go to sleep and wake up at a reasonable time, write a schedule that is varied and includes time for work as well as self-care.

2. Dress for the social life you want.
Put on bright colors to cheer your mood.

3. Get out at least once a day, for at least thirty minutes.
If you are at high risk, open the windows and blast the fan. Fresh air can lift spirits.

4. Find some time to move each day, for at least thirty minutes.
If all else fails, turn on music and have a dance party.

5. Reach out to others at least once daily, for at least thirty minutes.

6. Stay hydrated and eat well.
Challenge yourself to learn how to cook something new.

7. Develop a self-care tool kit.
It should contain something for each of your senses. You can supply your own tools, but here are some examples:
    Touch – a soft blanket
    Taste – hot chocolate

  Sight – photos of vacations
  Hearing – comforting music
  Smell – lavender oil
  Movement – rocking chair
  Comforting pressure – weighted blanket

8. **Spend time playing with children if they are in your home.**

9. **Give everyone the benefit of the doubt.**
 Everyone is doing the best they can.

10. **Find your own retreat space where you can be alone.**

11. **Expect behavioral issues in children and respond gently.**

12. **Focus on safety and attachment.**

13. **Lower expectations and practice radical self-acceptance.**

14. **Limit social media and COVID conversation, especially around children.**

15. **Notice the good in the world, the helpers.**

16. **Help others.**
 Find ways, big and small, to give back to others.

17. Find something you can control and control the heck out of it.
Organize your bookshelf, purge your closet, group your toys, for example.

18. Find a long-term project to dive into.
Put together a huge jigsaw puzzle or some such endeavor.

19. Engage in repetitive movements and left-right movements.
These movements, like knitting, coloring, or running, can be self-soothing.

20. Find an expressive art.
See how relieved you can feel by doing something like singing, drawing, or dancing.

21. Find humor in each day.

22. Reach out for help.

23. Take your quarantine moment by moment.
Focus on whatever bite-size piece of challenge you can manage.

24. Remind yourself daily that this is temporary.

25. Find the lesson in it for you.
What needs to change in yourself, your home, your community, your nation, your world?

A Different Way of Seeing

We are being called to see ourselves and the world we live in as interrelated and continually changing. Our own personhood is *interpersonhood*. We are not in the world alone. When we interchange love and life, we create oneness of being with all that we are in contact with. Even suffering together pulls us into oneness of being.

A new creation is evolving. We do not know what the new creation will be. But, we can trust that we will be part of the new creation in one form or another. We may not like or understand what is unfolding, but we can be sure it is part of something we don't fully see yet. Nothing is random, only fully perceived or not. As author of *The Enlightenment Trilogy*, Jed McKenna puts it, "Whatever happens must be the best thing that *could* happen, because it is the thing that *does* happen. Ultimately, the only criteria we have by which to determine what is best is what occurs" (McKenna 2010, Book Three, 205).

We will be going more deeply into this new way of seeing and being in future chapters. For now, focusing on the following exercises can help you to prepare yourself for the new way of being.

Co-creating Together Exercise

1. **Take time to appreciate.**
   Take time to appreciate what we typically take for granted.
   Think of loved ones and express your appreciation to them.
   Think of friends and give them a call.
   Think of your blessings and feel grateful.

2. **Find humor in what is happening in the world.**
   What is the treasure to be found at the grocery store? Toilet paper and eggs. And the internet is filled with cartoons, films, and memes to make you laugh.

3. **Slow down.**
   Have wonderful conversations with people.
   Savor the beauty of nature.
   Give thanks for the singing of birds.
   Take time to love.

4. **Speak the truth.**
   Where there is panic, offer patience.
   Where there is suffering, give acts of kindness.

4-7-8 Breathing Exercise

Here is a wonderful breathing exercise from Dr. Gregory Scott Brown, director of the Center for Green Psychiatry and affiliate faculty at the University of Texas Dell Medical School, who was reporting for Medscape Psychiatry on Facebook, April 7, 2020.

> **Find a quiet space.**
> **Bring your attention to your breath.**
> **Take a deep inhale, count to 4, hold, count to 7.**
> **On a long cleansing exhale, count to 8.**

Dr. Brown writes, "The long exhale is critically important because research has shown that it can help activate the parasympathetic nervous system as well as increased GABA levels in our brain, and even promote alpha-wave activity on EEG – all indicators that our body is in a calm and relaxed state."

Part II

New Image of a Human Being

This section teaches how we establish our identities in the first half of life, in the second half of life, and how we get to I AM.

Chapter 4

The First Half of Life: Establishing an Identity of "Me"

> *No one is born hating another person ... People must learn to hate, and if they can learn to hate, they can be taught to love. For love comes more naturally to the human heart than its opposite.*
>
> **Nelson Mandela**
> *Long Walk to Freedom*

The first half of life teaches us that we are different from everybody else. This essential and important identity of "me" determines—physically, psychologically, and spiritually—what we believe to be true about our Being and the world. Hopefully, what we learn is taught to us with love, as Nelson Mandela encourages in the quote above. But even when we are not taught with love, we can get back to love because our brains continue to reorganize throughout our lives.

How we learn in the first half of life can be explained neurologically, psychologically, and biologically. Neurologically, human beings have nerve cells in our brains called mirror neurons, which equip us to imitate others (Blakemore & Decety 2001; di Pellegrino et al. 1992; Gallese 2001; Gallese et al. 1996, 2002; Mukamel et al. 2010; Rizzolati et al. 1996; Rizzolatti & Craighero 2004). Through body-to-body knowing we understand *what* others are doing and *why* they are doing it. This is because when we see another do something, the mirror neurons in our brains activate as if we were performing the act ourselves—even though we aren't acting.

Psychologically human beings begin life with an inborn capacity that promotes attachment to our caregivers (Bowlby 1969, 1973, 1988). The types of attachment we form with our caregivers have been categorized (Ainsworth et al. 1978, Main & Solomon 1986). These social attachments contribute to the development of attachment patterns that become internal working models of how we experience others and life in general (Mikulincer & Shaver 2010).

Biologically, human beings have a binary operating system built right into the structure of their brains. Ian McGilchrist writes, "…the brain has to attend to the world in two completely different ways, and in so doing to bring two different worlds into being" (2009, 31). In the right half of the brain, the world is experienced as a network of interdependencies, where we are deeply connected to one another and to all of nature. The left half of the brain interprets the world as separate and disconnected entities which are sorted into groups that determine how we understand what we see.

The "either/or" system of the left hemisphere is a way of making sense of the world by dividing the world into self and other. One of the most important tasks of early childhood is learning how to run this operating system. This is the way we form our identity as distinct "me." It is important in that it enables us to read, calculate, and think objectively and critically.

Our distinct "me" results from how our mirror neurons imitated actions that our caregivers provided us, from how our attachment patterns laid the template for our future relationships, and from how we learned to use our left brain hemisphere to run our "either/or" operating system. But this identity doesn't see the full picture of oneness; it sees dualistically: me and you.

This incomplete picture becomes our adult brain's default setting for our personality and for our relationship patterns. It contributes to our adult view of *our* world, not *the* world and what is *actual, real, and true*. So what do we need to do to be able to see the world as an interconnected oneness?

Preparing to See the World as Actual, Real, and True

First realize what is *not* true. Everything that tells us that we are separate from everything else is false. Answering questions and solving problems will not bring us to seeing what is true reality. Reality is what remains when we stop believing in the old paradigm of disconnection and separation. Our essential Being remains when we stop believing in all the characteristics of "me" which we learned early in life, realizing that we are so much more.

An excellent story about man's pursuit of the actual, real, and true is Herman Melville's *Moby-Dick*. The book is Captain Ahab's log of the voyage he took to kill the white whale, Moby-Dick. Many have thought that Captain Ahab's pursuit of Moby-Dick reflects his gradual descent into madness, but I agree with Jed McKenna, who says that the story portrays Captain Ahab's life-and-death struggle to destroy what prevents his freedom to be the essential Being he was born to be (McKenna 2010, Book Two).

What characterizes Captain Ahab's journey to see the world as actual, real, and true according to McKenna? (1) He has purity of intent. He has one goal and one goal only: kill the white whale. (2) Captain Ahab has undergone a death/rebirth experience when Moby Dick severed one of his legs in a previous encounter. (3) Captain Ahab has no desired outcome except to go farther in pursuit of his freedom. (4) He is amoral; in other words, he is neither moral nor immoral. The pursuit of our essential being has nothing to do with morality. It has everything to do with our desire to reconnect with and live in the freedom of the energy of love. (5) Captain Ahab has lost a significant part of himself—his leg, which he can never get back. In addition, he knows that the "me" of his early years is gone forever. (6) He is only drawn to kill Moby-Dick because doing so removes the obstacle to his reclaiming his essential Being and living freely in the energy of his inherent nature. Moby-Dick is a demon he has created. To awaken, Captain Ahab must slay the demon.

We all create our own demons. To awaken, we must slay them. In the process, the same characteristics that defined Captain Ahab's journey may characterize your journey to see the world holistically. As you shed what is unreal about who "me" is, you will arrive at the real "us." As you release the old, you will be able to embrace the new. In other words, as we embrace the new, "our ever-growing capacity for love and freedom—find their source in the elegant mystery that is our home and our destiny" (Cannato 2010, 74).

Before turning to the next chapter, try the following two exercises. The mirror exercise can show you something important about a pitfall of living from a "me" identity. The diminishing fear exercise can help you reach a physiological state that will promote your journey into the second half of your life.

Mirror Exercise

🐚 This exercise is from Michael Brown's book *The Presence Process: A Journey Into Present Moment Awareness*, Revised Edition. Vancouver, Canada: Namaste Publishing, 2010, 218-219.

"*Please go to a mirror, do this exercise, and observe.* Stand in front of the mirror and behave as if you are trying to get something from the reflection by taking from it. You will see clearly that 'getting by taking' is the cause of our experience of lack.

When we feel lack in any aspect of our experience, it's because somewhere or somehow we are attempting to get what we want by taking from others whatever we perceive to be lacking in ourselves.

Here is an important realization to digest: Our wanting, which is driven by our unintegrated emotional charge, leads us to believe that what we seek in order to feel satisfied is something solid and tangible—money, a car, a new house, a position in the workplace. But it isn't. It's never the 'thing' that we are really after, but *the resonance associated with possessing the thing.*"

Diminishing Fear Exercise

🐚 Stop imagining what will make you feel better. Instead, bring gratitude throughout your day. Imaginings will not decrease your fear but gratitude will.

Feel gratitude for all the gifts of life. This releases fear by transmuting it back into its original form of radiant light.

See world threats such as the COVID-19 pandemic as invitations to awaken and enter into the vibration of unity consciousness with Mother Nature, which is more than the roles and identities that we think we are.

Experience world threats such as the COVID-19 pandemic as calls to reconnect with yourself, the Universe, and the flow of nature's energy.

Respond to whatever happens with "thank you."

Be exuberant in the moment; bask in its joy.

Chapter 5

The Second Half of Life: Establishing an Identity of "Us"

> *To live from the inner depth of love, as persons in evolution, is to live with purpose and direction not as an "I" but as a "we," a collective whole.*
>
> **Ilia Delio**
> *The Unbearable Wholeness of Being*

The second half of life calls us to transcend the identity of "me," growing into the fullness of our deeper nature, an identity of "us," with awareness that we and all creation are one. As spiritual teacher Eckhart Tolle says, "You need nature as your teacher to help you reconnect with Being. But not only do you need nature, it also needs you. You are not separate from nature" (Tolle 2003, 84). Indeed, we are one with all creation.

To become truly aware of this, we must shift to a different basis of perception than the one we used to form our identity of "me." We must see what physicists see: that the foundational nature of reality is relational. That is, everything – including human beings – is in relationship with everything else. And personhood is not static; it is dynamic and interactive. We are continually in a process of coming to be.

How we learn to see in this new way in the second half of life can be explained neurologically, psychologically, and biologically, in the same way that learning in the first half of life was explained in the previous chapter. Before we begin, though, I want to emphasize that the mechanisms I am about to describe are all working in the first half of life, as well, and the mechanisms explained in the previous chapter are all working in the second half of life, too. Humans are complex beings!

That said, let's turn to neurology. Neurologically, human beings—like all mammals—have nervous systems that automatically prepare our bodies for social communication. Stephen W. Porges, Distinguished University Scientist at Indiana University and discoverer of the Polyvagal Neurological System, writes, "Polyvagal Theory emphasizes that the neural circuits that support social behavior and emotional regulation are available only when the nervous system deems the environment safe and that these circuits are involved in health, growth, and restoration" (2017, 47). In other words, we need a safe environment in order to establish an identity of "us." If the environment is not safe, our nervous systems will automatically prepare us for fight/flight or freezing, and these physiological states can prevent us from growing into our identity of "us."

Psychologically, intersubjectivity is the starting point for human development. Intersubjectivity is interpersonal communion expressed in acts of co-creating (Zlatev et al. 2008). There are four stages of intersubjectivity.

1. Primary intersubjectivity can be seen in newborns as young as forty-two minutes old, who imitate another's smile or tongue protrusion (Meltzoff 2011). This motor and emotional two-way attuning between others gives birth to our earliest sense of identity—our body identity (Gallese & Sinigaglia 2010).

2. Secondary intersubjectivity is a three-way engagement where an object is the focus of joint attention and emotional referencing within a trusting relationship between infant and caregiver (Trevarthen 2005). It appears from about nine months of age. An example of secondary intersubjectivity would be an infant and dog, side by side and looking at the same person, each sticking out its tongue.

3. Tertiary intersubjectivity expresses collaborative engagement. It is attained in the second year of life when toddlers can engage in symbolic conversation, can share goals with others, and can share unspoken intentions (Meltzoff 2011). An example of tertiary intersubjectivity would be a toddler and father walking together side by side on a path that is their shared goal with the unspoken intention of completing their walk.

4. A fourth level of intersubjectivity—**understanding minds**—is achieved in year four of life (Allman et al. 2005). Now children can understand directly what the other person is doing, why he or she is doing it, and how he or she feels about the situation (Gallese 2011). All of these levels of intersubjectivity can be used to help us see that we are each a small part of all creation.

Biologically, we are born with the capacity to perceive oneness, but the goal of establishing "me" in the first half of life required us to focus our attention on our left brain hemisphere's operating system. Now, in the second half of life, we must choose to learn how to run the oneness operating system of our right brain hemisphere. All forms of meditative practices (Hinduism: Yoga; Islam: Sufism;

Judaism: Kabbalah; Christianity: Contemplative Prayer) have disciplines aimed to train us to see from the perspective of oneness. They teach us to see that one is not one, nor two, but both one and two. An example of seeing oneness is seeing that the wave and the ocean are both one and two.

Love is the Tie that Binds Us

Here I am reminded of Madeleine L'Engle's best-selling novel, *A Wrinkle in Time*, which is really a cosmic quest of love. The novel portrays the love of husband, astrophysicist Dr. Jack Murry and his wife, the love of these two parents for their children, the love of their teenage daughter, Meg for her neighbor, Calvin O'Keefe, and the love of everyone by the Murry's son Charles Wallace. Love binds all of them together in their awareness of "Us" as beloved to each other.

His family knows that six-year-old Charles Wallace is special because he reads the thoughts of those who need him. Not only does he possess this special gift, but he also is untouched by what most in his environment consider important for their self worth. He lives true to his essence.

When Dr. Jack Murry disappears, Charles Wallace, Meg, and Calvin O'Keefe travel to a distant planet, guided by three extraterrestrial beings, Mrs. Whatsit, Mrs. Who, and Mrs. Which, where they encounter a society controlled by an evil force. By trusting each other and bonding under the force of love, they succeed in rescuing Dr. Murry.

It is particularly within Charles Wallace that the battle between love and evil is fought and won. He does not win the battle alone, however. It is Meg's love for Charles Wallace that destroys the hate regime and enables Charles Wallace to win his battle. Together they show readers how living from their essence along with being aware of their oneness, gives them power to come through diversity undamaged and alive.

Let's define love more explicitly: as a state of Being, not an emotion. In the words of writer Raimon Panikkar, "In phenomenological terms, love is a nondualistic experience ... Love is neither equality nor otherness, neither one nor two. Love requires differentiation without separation; it is a 'going' toward 'the other' that rebounds in a genuine 'entering' into oneself by accepting the other within one's bosom" (Panikkar 2004, 57).

In other words, reciprocal loving is how we know *who* another person is and how the other person knows *who* we are. When we are loved by another, we can see him or her in the mirror which love of the other has created in us. Thus, we know each other's identity by sharing our identities. Stated differently, "To live from the inner depth of love, ... is to live with purpose and direction not as an 'I' but as a 'we,' a collective whole" (Delio 2013, 112).

To experience this kind of love, we must learn to activate our oneness operating system. Once we can experience the oneness at the heart of being, it follows that love is our longing for oneness, for being one with all other. Indeed, love is the essence of our Being. Our connectedness to all creation is our fundamental reality.

How do we learn to run our oneness operating system? Those readers who have active meditative practices have already started the process. Those who have not yet begun a meditative practice might want to try one or both of the exercises that follow.

Body Scan Exercise

🌀 This exercise is adapted from Resmaa Menakem's book *My Grandmother's Hands: Racialized Trauma and the Pathway to Mending Our Hearts and Bodies*. Las Vegas, NV: Central Recovery Press, 2017, 158.

> Stand or sit comfortably. Now take a few breaths.
>
> Feel into your body. Where does it seem tight or uncomfortable in any way? Note each of these locations.
>
> Then, one location at a time, gently press your hand against the uncomfortable spot.
>
> For thirty to forty-five seconds, simply experience that gentle pressure.
>
> Then rub the spot, slowly and gently. If this feels good, keep rubbing for thirty to sixty seconds. If it doesn't, stop.
>
> Do this for each part of your body where there is pain, constriction, or distress.
>
> Use this activity whenever a part of your body feels uncomfortable.

Walking Exercise

This exercise is modified from Richard Rohr and Mike Morrell's book *The Divine Dance: The Trinity and Your Transformation*. New Kensington, PA: Whitaker House, 2016, 202.

1. **Go for a walk alone and in silence.**
   Return alone and in silence.
2. **Do your seeing on your own and own it as your own.**

3. **Note any thoughts, emotions, and sensations.**
   They can be your teacher.

4. **Goal-lessness is your goal.**
   The journey is the total destination.

5. **Place one foot lovingly and intentionally in front of the other.**

6. **Take no books or journals.**
   Just look.

7. **Do not hope to find something profound or meaningful to say.**
   Any expectation is a disappointment waiting to happen.

8. **It is what it is, and that is your teacher.**

Chapter 6

Getting to I AM

> *Nature can do nothing other than be itself, and in being itself it is truly free.*
>
> **Ilia Delio**
> *The Unbearable Wholeness of Being*

While nature can only be itself, human beings often do not know their I AM and therefore are not truly free. To know I AM is to be in touch with one's central core energy. Energy is activity. I AM is activity.

Our I AM is what is behind all those descriptions we have of ourselves. For example, in my case, my I AM is quite independent of: I am a woman, I am a retired psychiatrist, I am a writer, I am 5 foot 2 inches, I am an Enneagram 8, etc., etc. etc. The problem is that without all the attributes that distinguish us from other beings, our I AM looks like nothing at all, as No-Self, as a big zero. However, this sense of No-Self is simply the last of our perceptions of whatever can define or describe our self in relation to others. Once these perceptions are gone, we are free to experience I AM as the true reality of our existence.

Four Characteristics of I AM

Beatrice Bruteau, in her book *The Grand Option: Personal Transformation and a New Creation*, describes four characteristics of I AM.

> 1. "It must be experienced from the inside, by actually *being* it. It is sheer I AM, without adding "I am this," or "I am that." No, only "I am who I am" (113).

Experiencing our selves in this way is a new way of knowing. It is knowing by uniting with and becoming one with who we truly are. This knowledge by communion enables us to experience ourselves as active, as the energy of living, as Being. In the words of spiritual teacher, Eckhart Tolle, "Being can be felt, but it can never be understood mentally" (Tolle 2001, 8).

> 2. Our "... formless existence-self is active, not passive" (115).

Our I AM is *being* love because what love *is* is the outflowing energy that unites us with one another. "The more I give myself away in love, the more I become myself, because that's what I *am*, a lover" (118). Genuine loving action arises spontaneously and freely from within us when we are living I AM.

> 3. When the dualism of subject and object has been transcended and we live I AM, then there is no longer a distinction between "me" and "my environment" (119).

When we live I AM, our "consciousness, ... coincides with its own act of existing ... and one is aware of unity with the whole. ... [In the context of I AM, the word *person* takes on new meaning.] Person ... refers to the living one who ... is simply the act of existing as a flowing fountain of consciousness" (119).

I awoke to this fact a few days ago. I had plans for the day. I was going to exercise, do some reading, work on this book and perhaps go to the grocery store. Then, my computer crashed. Who knows why or how, but there went my plans. I could have chosen to do one or more of the above activities. I chose to call Apple Support who, hopefully, could get my computer back up and working. The call took over three hours. That's my life and probably yours too. Some sort of plan for life is good, but we also have to be ready for anything. We have to balance our sense of where we are and where we are going with an absolute openness to what the world might have in store for us. This is truly "unity with the whole".

Would you like to visualize what "unity with the whole" is like? Imagine a fidget spinner toy. At rest, the toy looks like three round protrusions connected by a central round spinner. When you spin the spinner, however, the toy looks like one whole spinning object.

4. After ridding ourselves of all the self-descriptions learned in the first half of our lives, after freeing ourselves to enter into the nondual dance of life, we turn outward to live our lives in the fullness of love.

Once we realize I AM, we can then bring our active energy into the world where it can transform human consciousness, which is necessary if humankind is not to destroy itself.

Bruteau's four characteristics of I AM are very similar to what Alexander J. Shaia, Ph.D. delineates as the four paths of transformation (2006). First there is the decision to embark on the journey, withdrawing from our restricted self to actually experience I AM. Second, there is the experience of following the path, analogous to realizing our nature as lovers. Third is reflection on arrival at the place, which is the awareness of profound union. And, fourth is the return home to integrate revelations into every day life, which is turning our faces outward again in the creative process of incarnation.

Judy Cannato (2010) also describes four essential characteristics of I AM, but from a different perspective. First, we are self-reflective beings who know that we know. Second, we ask questions; we quest for knowledge. Third, we love. And, fourth we live in a milieu of freedom. The new consciousness that is emerging invites us to engage all four characteristics on behalf of all life.

Another Person's Experience of I AM

Author Bernadette Roberts describes her experience of I AM in her book entitled *The Experience of No-Self: A Contemplative Journey* (1993). Remember that at the beginning of this chapter we acknowledged that the experience of I AM can seem like No-Self. So, I am equating Roberts' experience of No-Self with an experience of I AM.

Like Bruteau, Roberts acknowledges that it is basically impossible to explain what life is like without all the "this and thats" which we use to describe ourselves. Instead, she says that I AM can only be experienced rather than understood. The experience "is a continuous waking state in which the physical organism remains sensitive, responsive, and totally unimpaired. When fully adjusted to the dimension of no self, nothing is found to be missing or wanting. It is only in the encounter with other selves that a self or affective system is a reminder of what *was*" (181).

For Roberts, the experience of I AM was such that each moment contained within itself the appropriate action without any need for thought, feeling, will or energy. She called the experience *doing*. In her words, "… when there is no longer any separation between act and being, then and only then, is there 'doing.' It is not easy to get used to doing without a doer; indeed, the very thought of it is unthinkable. Yet the body functions this way all the time. No one is telling the heart to beat or how our liver must function. So who is doing this, who is in charge here? We call this the 'wisdom of the body,' which is a good example of doing without a doer" (116-177).

Furthermore, she noticed that though there was no change in her personal relationships, there was a change in her way of knowing others. "Where before I had seen the individual first, and his true Other second, now the Other is seen first—and the individual? Well, I do not really see him at all, not at least as before. Instead of a self I see ideas, behaviors, decisions, struggles, and much more, but I do not see a self because it has been paled or effaced by what is really there" (193). Her relationships, when she experienced I AM, existed without problems because there was an intrinsic bond of love between all that existed. She defined love, not as an emotion, but as a strong desire for good for others as she desired for herself.

Now that you have heard from some who have experienced I AM, would you like to experience your I AM? To realize our relation with one another as mutual indwelling (I am in you and you are in me), we must first learn to identify with our own central core energy of existence. Doing so changes our perception of ourselves. Try this exercise:

Changing Your Perception of Yourself Exercise

This exercise is adapted from Beatrice Bruteau's book *The Grand Option: Personal Transformation and a New Creation* Notre Dame, IN: University of Notre Dame Press, 2001, 160.

> Sit with yourself in the experience of being "I am such-and-such." Use varying descriptors to identify yourself. If you said "I am fat," say "I am thin," and so on. Identify with existing in each way. Discover that the concrete sense "I AM" remains stable despite any changes of descriptor.
>
> Now remove the descriptors altogether, beginning with the physical ones and working gradually toward the more interior ones. Remain centered in the sense "I AM" as you do this. When all the descriptors have been removed, notice that your sense of identity will be profoundly centered in the "I AM" alone and will be immediately aware of itself as intrinsically living and luminous.

Part III

Living in Communion

This final section of *Our Changing World* focuses on claiming our transcendent self, entering oneness conscious, and maintaining hope in times of turmoil.

Chapter 7

The Transcendent Self

> *... when we know that we are love, we don't need to work at being loving toward others. Instead, we just have to be true to ourselves, and we become instruments of loving energy, which touches everyone we come into contact with.*
>
> **Anita Moorjani**
> *Dying to Be Me*

Our I AM has also been called our transcendent self. Our transcendent self is what we experience when we let go all the descriptions of ourselves that we learned in the first half of our lives. It is our core self-giving, universally loving, energy-center. Our transcendent self is simply our process, our activity, our doing.

What we do is love. We are lovers. A lover *is* the act of loving. The act of loving establishes differentiation of our transcendent self simultaneously with union because each loving person is thoroughly "in" each other loving person. Each person is seeing with the other's eyes, hearing with the other's ears, feeling with the other's heart, and uniting with the other's actions. In other words, two persons "are distinct because they are their own acts of existing" and each person unites "with the other [so] as to live in the other's own life" (Bruteau 2001, 120). But even in unity each person knows that "I am I" because this is what each person is.

What a different world it would be if we could all connect with this transcendent self, with our loving energy, our I AM! So how do we do it?

Four Steps to Connect with our Loving Energy as explained by Beatrice Bruteau

Remember that we are talking about transformation—our changing world and our changing being. We are talking about our world moving toward our personal I AM and toward our communal oneness consciousness, so the first step for connecting with our loving energy will probably not surprise you.

> **1. "Understand how evolutionary development of the universe has been working and can be expected to continue"** (Bruteau 2001, 14).

The Big Bang, the great flaring forth of creativity, brought forth our universe over 13.7 billion years ago. The intentionality toward life was expressed from the first moment. "In its latent potential, the embodied person that you are at this very moment—all the constituents that would eventually come together into the person that is you—was present in the Big Bang" (Cannato 2006, 43). We live, and our world has always lived, in the midst of immense creativity.

The universe is still expanding. We are still evolving toward our unique transcendent selves and our communal oneness consciousness. The urge to transform, to love and be loved, resides at the center of life.

2. **"Open ourselves to being loved *as persons*"** (Bruteau 2001, 14).

When another person loves us, our energy is activated. When all our energies interact, we can all become new beings—the beings we are meant to be. We are *"inter independent"* (Panikkar 2004, 67) beings who are able to know each other by opening ourselves to love. Yet, each of us participates in the same consciousness in our own unique way. Thus, we keep our own unique personhood even in becoming new beings. Life is mysterious.

3. **"To the extent that we have received love, we can love others"** (Bruteau 2001, 14).

We can share our self with another freely because now we realize we can transcend and no longer be trapped in the reaction patterns of our first half of life. We can be self-giving in love by the creative freedom inherent in transcendence. Love brought us into transcendent new being, which can bring others into transcendent new beings. This goes beyond what unions on a biological, emotional or social level can create. It is love given without any motive that has reference to oneself; rather, it wills the good of the other. And, it freely chooses where to concentrate its energy at any given time.

4. **"Take care that our behavior and decisions for action . . . embody the sentiments we are learning to experience in these loving attitudes"** (Bruteau 2001, 15).

When we live from our transcendent selves, our behavior and decisions are not reactions or responses to previously existing situations or values; they arise within us as their first source. We are free to love others regardless of their behavior. We give ourselves completely and unite with the loved one so as to know, understand, and feel the beloved. We experience our beloved *as actually being* ourself. This is experiencing selfhood in a new way—as interpersonhood. We are persons in process together.

Connecting with our core loving energy, with our transcendent energy of existence, with our I AM, connects us with the energy that began our universe. Now we can flow into the world with creative freedom. But inner freedom can be frightening. It requires letting go of our desire for safety and security, and this can take a long time. It is a process that requires brutal honesty and constant vigilance. It requires that we remember that we are love.

Creative Freedom

Freedom is the hallmark of being human. What is freedom? "Freedom is our capacity to seek meaning and stake our lives on what we have discovered" (Cannato 2010, 77). Living in creative freedom allows us to live into the lives of others. In other words, each of us understands the Other in direct proportion to our knowing that the Other is ourself. The Other becomes more you the more you love it.

It is our own doing, our own initiative, to freely indwell in others. When others live in creative freedom and indwell us, our location of selfhood changes from "me" to "we." We are process persons, persons of radiating energy who are creating community. We are intended to live in unity and community.

As an example of indwelling in others, I recall John Grisham's bestseller *A Time to Kill* in which a black man, Carl Lee Hailey, is on trial in a small Mississippi town for killing the two redneck brothers who molested his small ten year old daughter, leaving her with a severe concussion, broken bones, and the inability to ever bear children. Carl Lee Hailey's white lawyer, Jake Brigance, needs to convince a white jury not to condemn his client, because he knew that a white jury would set the white molesters free. In the 1996 Warner Brothers movie version of the novel, the lawyer encourages the jury to indwell the murderer. He does so by walking the jury through the molestation and then finishes by asking the jury to close their eyes and imagine that it is a white child who is molested. As a result, the jury votes to set Carl Lee Hailey free. This example is not to condone killing, but to show that what we see when we see from within another person may be different from what society dictates that we see.

Persons living in community can realize their relationships with one another in participatory consciousness, just as these jury members were able to do. But before delving more fully into participatory consciousness, I encourage you to take time to become aware of any sense of loss you might be feeling. Even though connecting with I AM and living from your transcendent self can be exhilarating, there may also be a sense of loss of what was familiar.

Loss of the sense of self defined by color, creed, profession, or any of the familiar ways we learned in the first half of life deserves to be grieved, because even though these definitions still exist, they are not as important as they were before. Every step in the journey is a loss of the old "me." As long as there is more to lose, there are more steps to take until everything is lost.

Achieving creative freedom is a process of constant becoming, a process of loss and renewal, a movement toward clearer seeing of what is true. It is a process from I-It and I-Thou to I-I relationships. More and more clearly, we see that no one and no part is greater or lesser. No part is apart; every part contains the whole.

It is important to take time to grieve all losses. Only by fully grieving will we be released from the past and ready for experiencing creative freedom. The following exercise can help you to sense any grief you may be feeling.

Becoming Aware of Grief Exercise

1. Take time to be quiet and let yourself feel how you have changed.
Are you uncertain about how life will unfold for you now that you live from more freedom to love?
Do you sense a loss of safety? A loss of normalcy?
What other sensations arise in your quiet?

2. Stay in the present.
Breathe.
Name five things in the room: a computer, a telephone, a chair, a desk, a lamp—or whatever you see where you are. Staying in the present is as simple as that.

3. Experience grief in your own way.
If you allow your feelings to happen, they will happen in an orderly way. Feel them all: denial, anger, bargaining, sadness, and acceptance. Then, keep going.

Chapter 8

Oneness Consciousness

Love is the energy that empowers union; union generates new creation, and each new creation is more whole and united in love— more personal.

Ilia Delio
The Unbearable Wholeness of Being

Oneness consciousness is a consciousness of whole persons, persons who have found their I AM and embraced their transcendent selves. It is a consciousness that values each person, a consciousness that reflects the love of whole persons uniting in community and sharing their life energies with one another. It is a consciousness that sees the world in constant flux. Twentieth century paleontologist, Pierre Teilhard de Chardin calls oneness consciousness "collective consciousness." According to American theologian Ilia Delio, Teilhard claimed that collective consciousness is the very basis of personhood—the I AM—and we can only find our I AM by uniting together. (Delio 2016, 113). We are all one, connected to one another and to all creation.

When each person gives themselves entirely to each fellow person, then each one's being is fully involved in every other one's being. This means that each person becomes part of the energy of the whole community and at the same time remains unique in each person's wholeness. Oneness consciousness is "simultaneously one and many, both the unity and the multiplicity being generated by the same act, the act of projecting life-giving energies toward fellow members of the community..." (Bruteau 2001, 170).

Dualistic	Nondualistic
Thinking: rational, analytical, linear, reductionistic	**Thinking:** intuitive, synthesizing, integrative, holistic
Values: competitive, quantitative, domination over, expansive	**Values:** cooperative, quality is better, partnership and conservation
Vision: seeing two things as two	**Vision:** seeing two things as one
Consciousness: living in the past or future	**Consciousness:** living in the present without splitting or dividing, without judgment, analysis or resistance

Oneness consciousness, then, is a consciousness of whole persons and it values each one equally. It gives birth to persons by mutual affirmation. And it sees people as radically free and responsible doers rather than the sum of static characteristics.

Susanne Cook-Greuter, Ed.D's studies of consciousness posited that 10% of adults remain in the preconventional stage of consciousness that most people traverse before age twelve; 80% of adults reach the conventional stage of consciousness where subject and object are considered distinct and that by analyzing the parts one can figure out the whole. And 10% of adults reach a postconventional and a postpostconventional stage, two rarely-described stages that are the focus of Cook-Greuter's research (Cook-Greuter 1999/2010).

She describes this 10% of adults as functioning with Unitive Consciousness, and categorizes these adults into two stages. Where she uses the term **Self-definition**, I am taking the liberty of renaming **Self** as **Being**, which is less dualistic language.

Unitive Consciousness

Stage I: Construct-aware	**Stage II: Unitive**
Being-Understanding: can register paradoxes in human nature	**Being-Understanding:** considers all persons as part of ongoing humanity fulfilling evolutionary destiny
Being-Experience: the person has a foot in two worlds (1) the self as separate (2) all life as interconnected	**Being-Experience:** the person feels embedded in all creation
Being-Sense: can hold contradictions without needing to resolve them	**Being-Sense:** everything that happens is part of the evolutionary process

This research gives helpful empirical support to the fact that unitive consciousness is indeed the kind of consciousness toward which human beings are evolving.

Personhood within Oneness Consciousness

🐚 Here is an example of someone who experienced personhood within oneness consciousness: Eben Alexander, M.D., a noted neurosurgeon, suffered bacterial meningitis that led to a seven-day coma. On the seventh day of coma his doctors held a family conference where they gave him a 2% chance of survival and a zero chance of recovery to any sort of normal daily routine. However, against these odds, he did wake up in the Intensive Care Unit where he was being kept alive. After awakening, his language came back over hours and days; life memories returned over the next five weeks; all prior knowledge of physics, chemistry and neuroscience returned over about two months. During coma he experienced ultrareal deep memories of a realm that was more fundamental than our earthly realm. This realm "was the source of *all*, the ultimate nonduality of pure oneness ... [where he] encountered the power of infinite unconditional love, the very *feeling* of that ineffable love" (Alexander and Newell 2017, 11).

The realm he experienced was oneness consciousness: "the ultimate nonduality of pure oneness." Furthermore, this experience changed his personhood to one open to "ineffable love." Within oneness consciousness, personhood is defined as a free sharing of our loving selves. We are like magnets, relating to each other's vibrations. We are mutually exchanging energy and love. We are freely indwelling others and others are indwelling us. We need not like each other, but we prize each other and promote each other's unique I AM. Everyone is loved and everyone is unique. Everyone must belong to constitute the whole because each person brings a unique I AM, which only that person can bring.

As Bruteau has said, in the process of profound and total sharing, each Person thoroughly indwells or lives in each other Person, and that is what makes oneness consciousness (Bruteau 2001, 67). The old dualistic we/they consciousness must be transformed into oneness consciousness. Dualistic consciousness has served us well throughout our human history, enabling us to survive and spread. But now life is urging us to move from a MeWorld where human relationships are predominantly one of domination, into a WeWorld where human relationships are increasingly ones of giving ourselves and our life energies into the lives of each other. This, I believe, is what the election of Donald Trump to President of the United States is signaling: as hypothesized in Chapter 1, we are in a worldwide movement toward a paradigm that embraces the interconnected oneness of the universe. This is what the COVID-19 Pandemic is calling us to. None of us is safe unless all of us is safe. We are all in these experiences of crisis together.

"Like all great shifts in evolution, this projected elevation of our consciousness can be expected to be a massive, radical transformation that, while it is a kind of 'quantum leap' in each individual in whom it happens, shows up in whole populations only very gradually over a long period of time" (Bruteau 2001, 62). And, for this transformation to occur at all, it requires all our freely given conscious participation. We each must choose to allow our consciousness to be transformed. The world is calling us to participate.

Five Qualities Needed to Sustain our World

These qualities are adapted from sociologist and activist Parker J. Palmer, Ph.D. (2011/2014, 44-45).

1. **"We must understand that we are all in this together."**
   We humans are profoundly interconnected. We are dependent on and accountable to one another.

2. **"We must develop an appreciation of the value of 'otherness.'"**
   The stranger has much to teach us if we are willing to learn. There are creative possibilities in our differences if we can embrace them.

3. **"We must cultivate the ability to hold tensions in life-giving ways."**
   Life is full of contradictions. If we can embrace them, they can open us to new understandings of ourselves and our world that can generate energy and new life.

4. **"We must generate a sense of personal voice and energy."**
   We can trust our voice to speak our version of truth. Then, we must check and correct our version by listening to the truth of others.

5. **"We must strengthen our capacity to create community."**
   The companionship of two or three kindred spirits can give us courage to speak and act for justice. I like this definition of justice: Justice "… is love approximated, a balance of power among competing groups" (Cone 2011/2013, 33).

   All change requires loss of the old. Transforming into oneness consciousness requires loss of many false and superfluous certainties upon which we have built our daily schedules and our very lives. I encourage you to take time now to grieve these losses. The following coping exercise can be of help.

Coping with Grief Exercise

🐚 This exercise is my adaptation of some internet material on David Kessler, who co-wrote with Elizabeth Kübler-Ross *On Grief and Grieving: Finding Meaning through the Five Stages of Loss*. He has recently written his own book *Finding Meaning: The Sixth Stage of Grief* that had not yet been published at the time of this writing.

1) Acknowledge grief and understand the stages of grief. The five stages are not linear and may happen in any order. You may give your own examples of each stage. I have supplied examples relating to the pandemic.

Denial: The coronavirus may not happen where I live; it may not affect me.

Anger: The pandemic is making me stay home and taking away my activities.

Bargaining: So, if I social isolate for two weeks, I won't get the virus, right?

Sadness: I don't know when this will end.

Acceptance: This is happening. I have to figure out how to proceed.

2) Find balance in what you're thinking.

Instead of dwelling solely on the worst scenarios of what might happen, make yourself think of good scenarios. Don't try to make the bad scenarios go away; your mind is being protective. Just balance the bad scenarios with good ones.

3) **Be in the present.**

   Calm yourself and breathe. Acknowledge that in this moment you are okay.

4) **Let go what you can't control. Focus on what you can control.**

   In the event of the coronavirus, you can't control your neighbors. You can stay six feet away from them and you can wash your hands for twenty seconds.

5) **Stock up on compassion.**

   Be patient with others.

6) **Find meaning in what is happening.**

   That is what this book is all about.

Chapter 9

Hope in Times of Turmoil

*With kinship as the goal, other essential things fall into place . . .
were kinship our goal, we would no longer be promoting justice—
we would be celebrating it.*

Greg Boyle
Tattoos on the Heart

The election of Donald Trump to presidency of the United States in 2016, my own facing death and enduring suffering in 2019, and the COVID-19 pandemic of 2020, were three consecutive confrontations with turmoil for me. It took all three to wake me up to the fact that we are all one in our humanity. No one is more important than anyone else. We are each a small part of a much larger universal process. And we can be grateful to be a part of that process.

Unbinding Ourselves

How do we willingly participate in the larger mystery of life? We begin by accepting what is happening. We don't fight it; we don't run away from it; we don't blame others for it; we don't try to fix it.

We learn from it. One important lesson that I learned is that I am not in control. Like all human beings, I am just a part of some ultimate cosmic process that urges us to grow and become something new. "[T]he very meaning of being alive is to be constantly in the process of becoming a new creation" (Bruteau 2001, 147). We cannot know what the new creation will be, only that it will be.

As Greg Boyle says in the epigraph to this chapter, "With kinship as the goal, other essential things fall into place" but realizing that we are "us" is not easy. It entails the destabilizing of the security systems we learned in the first half of our lives, which maintain our identities of "me." This destabilization can bring us pain and suffering, but suffering is a fact of life. If we fight it, we cause ourselves more pain. If we accept it, our suffering is lightened, not because the destabilization is gone, but because we are "free internally of the situation" (Tolle 1999/2004, 83). When we transform our pain and suffering into acceptance and compassion, we do not transmit pain and suffering to others. This emotional transformation is what changes our consciousness and the world about us.

A Sufi tale captures the essence of accepting and transforming our suffering (Shah 1967, 23-24).

"A stream, from its source in far-off mountains, passing through every kind and description of countryside, at last reached the sands of the desert. Just as it had crossed every other barrier, the stream tried to cross this one, but it found that as fast as it ran into the sand its waters disappeared.

It was convinced, however, that its destiny was to cross this desert, and yet there was no way. Now a hidden voice, coming from the desert itself, whispered: 'The Wind crosses the desert, and so can the stream. ... You must allow the wind to carry you over, to your destination.'

But how could this happen? 'By allowing yourself to be absorbed in the wind.'

This idea was not acceptable to the stream. After all, it had never been absorbed before. It did not want to lose its individuality. And, once having lost it, how was one to know that it could ever be regained?

...

'But can I not remain the same stream that I am today?'

'You cannot ... remain so,' the whisper said. ... 'You are called what you are even today because you do not know which part of you is the essential one.'

When he heard this, certain echoes began to arise in the thoughts of the stream. Dimly, he remembered a state in which he—or some part of him, was it?—had been held in the arms of a wind. He also remembered—or did he?—that this was the real thing, not necessarily the obvious thing, to do.

And the stream raised his vapour into the welcoming arms of the wind, which gently and easily bore it upwards and along, letting it fall softly as soon as they reached the roof of a mountain, many, many miles away. ... [The stream] reflected, 'Yes, now I have learned my true identity.'

...

And that *is* why it is said that the way in which the Stream of Life is to continue on its journey is written in the Sands."

It is not outer events such as the stream's encounter with the desert or our emergency hospitalizations or pandemics that hurt us. What injures us is our defensive response to the emotions that these events arouse in us. "We can't change history but we can change the psyche's response to history" (Kalsched 2019). To do this, we must have a new experience where we learn that we can live through the turmoil, recover the feelings we warded off, and go forward in life having let our suffering pull us into oneness. In oneness, we can "reflect back to each other the love that [is felt] deep within, the love that comes with the realization of [our] oneness with all that is. This is the love that has no opposite" (Tolle 2001, 89).

If we want to change the world, we begin by changing ourselves.

Unbinding Others

Once we have unbound ourselves from the turmoil life brings, we can help others who are entombed by suffering. During the self-isolation of the COVID-19 pandemic, for example, I lived in a small gated community. It was heartening to see how reassuring the email connection between neighbors offering help and asking about each other's wellbeing was, and how it diminished the anxiety we all felt.

In addition to my specific experience, there are more general take-home messages about how to unbind others. I am going to offer five, which are my adaptations of what Richard Rohr, O.F.M offered in his daily meditations of April 6-10, 2020.

First: Life is hard, but understand that seeking the easy does not eliminate the difficult. Seeking ecstasy does not eliminate pain. Instead, experiencing the easy allows us stamina to suffer the difficult. Bathing in ecstasy empowers us to endure pain. However, "True joy is harder to access and even harder to hold onto than anger and fear" (Rohr, April 6, 2020).

Second: Although we are unimportant when viewed through the lens of eternity, we each are born with our own and only special gift to give the world. All we need to do is BE. When we do not cling to our neediness and hurt, the truth of our being shines into the world.

Third: Each person's life is about more than one's self. We are human *beings* more than human *doers* of any specific this or that. Each person's I AM is glorious, original and free. Live in gratitude and let the flow of love continue through you. "Love forever seeks more union, more being, more consciousness" (Delio 2013, 135).

Fourth: Since we can't control life and death, why waste energy trying to control smaller outcomes? Surrendering to the flow of the universe's energy does not mean giving in, being naïve, or stopping all thinking and planning. It's about giving ourselves away by inwardly opening to love, which allows love to flow through us to others. Giving up control to the flow of reality is the way to union and compassion.

Fifth: Death does not have the last word in our destiny. Love is our origin and love is our destiny. The love we bring into the world continues after we are gone. Love connotes something eternal and gratuitous. A small amount of love or gratitude can imprint a deep knowing in both giver and receiver.

Death and loss point us to the grief work discussed earlier in this book. In grief work, we hold our pain, look right at it, and learn from it. This softens our hearts and opens us to newly found compassion and understanding. If we could all do this, then we would be celebrating justice as the epigraph to this chapter acknowledges. Justice, remember, "is love approximated, a balance of power among competing groups" (Cone 2011/ 2013, 33). In other words, love in society is named justice.

None of these take-home messages are meant to minimize the world trauma that the pandemic has caused in terms of illness, death, and terror of physical proximity that will need to be addressed by professionals for years to come. Rather, they suggest tools that we can claim to help ourselves and those about us rebuild bridges to love and trust.

Seeing the Larger Picture

It is helpful to put what is happening in the world today into the larger picture of what has happened in the world since the beginning billions of years ago. Even extinction events in our past have generated good. As Joel Primack, professor of physics, writes, "Since the Cambrian explosion [approximately 541 million years ago when practically all major animal phyla started appearing in the fossil record], there have been at least five major extinction events, and each one was followed by major changes in the dominant sorts of living creatures. The most catastrophic was about 250 million years ago, and it killed almost all life on Earth and caused the extinction of more than 50 percent of marine families of organisms, and perhaps 90 percent of all species. This made way for both mammals and dinosaurs to evolve" (Primack and Abrams 2007, 219).

Seeing the larger picture can offer hope, which can change our way of seeing. Something dies but something new is born. As challenging as this may sound, I encourage you to look for new signs of being and becoming in the midst of chaotic times. Hope that is not tied to an outcome of things getting better but is the immediate experience of life becoming something new generates joy and satisfaction within us. Seeing the larger picture helps.

Realize that "[v]isible matter is only 0.5 percent of the total [matter of the universe]" (Primack and Abrams 2007, 114). Most of the matter of the universe is invisible. Likewise, most of us identify ourselves with fairly narrow categories—nationality, race, religion—but a wider sense of identity can yield a genuine connection to the universe and less conflicts between categories. Reality is demanding our wider sense of identity now.

Times of trial can be opportunities to choose what really matters and what passes away. Let the times of trial show all of us the false and superfluous certainties around which we have constructed our daily schedules, our projects, our habits and our priorities. Then, perhaps, we can accept the true gift of who we each already are even if it does not conform to some image of who we think we *ought* to be. If we can do so, we will also find our authentic path of service in the world. As activist, Parker J. Palmer, writes, "…Every journey, honestly undertaken, stands a chance of taking us toward the place where our deep gladness meets the world's deep need" (Palmer 2000, 36).

Of one thing we can all be sure: nothing ever stays the same. Life is always evolving. Life, in any extreme, challenges us to discover what we really live by and who we really are.

May you have the courage to change and grow in love. And may we all grow and change in love together.

Postscript

Racial Unrest 2020

> *America is headed for increased racial conflict and violence. There is no escape because the white man is determined to preserve injustice and we are determined that justice is ours by right and that we shall have it.*
>
> **Albert B. Cleage, Jr.**
> *The Black Messiah*

These words were written in 1989 by a black man for black people. They seem prophetic now.

I had just finished writing *Our Changing World* when George Floyd, an unarmed black man, was killed in Minneapolis police custody on May 25, 2020. Civil unrest began in the United States the next day, with multiple protests against racism and police brutality, and quickly spread throughout the world with thousands upon thousands of demonstrators, even in the midst of the pandemic. I could not let this book go to publication without addressing how civil unrest fits into *Our Changing World*.

Systemic Aggression

🐚 Racism belongs to what has been called systemic aggression, which includes such things as wars, terrorist attacks, the dismantling of ecosystems, obscene economic inequality, and potential nuclear catastrophe. Sound familiar? It should: systemic aggression has characterized our current century. It is becoming abundantly clear that our world is in crisis.

Just as Donald Trump's election to the presidency, my own personal health crisis, and the 2020 pandemic prompted startling realizations for me, so has this summer's racial unrest. Like many of you, I have always prided myself on my ability to embrace difference, and have believed that I am not racially prejudiced. I was a teenager in the 1950s; in high school I was active in the Brotherhood Presbyterian Church in Wichita, Kansas, involved in the cause of racial integration four years before the Montgomery, Alabama boycott of segregated city bus lines, and before the Reverend Martin Luther King, Jr. emerged as a leader for civil rights. I had always felt at the forefront of racial issues.

However, George Floyd's murder, and the racial unrest that followed, forced me to face how little I have been truly aware of racism. I recently read Howard Thurman's (1899-1981) autobiography and learned that he co-founded the first fully integrated church in America, Church of the Fellowship of All Peoples, in San Francisco, with his white co-pastor, Alfred Fisk, in 1944—long before the work I was involved with in the fifties. His autobiography, and his book *Jesus and the Disinherited*, helped me see through a black person's eyes what growing up in America does to people of color. It helped me realize that oppression is not what destroys people: it is the acceptance of oppression that destroys them. And it helped me see my own subtle contributions to oppression, if only in not being fully informed about conditions in America.

I don't believe that I am alone in this: many whites have a difficult time truly understanding the experiences of people of color, and can't really grasp the need for protest against inequality in our United States and in the world. Our current racial unrest urges us to awaken to the reality of systemic aggression and the role of the privileged and powerful in perpetuating these systems. This unrest is an invitation to rebuild our world. And we can start with our own personal transformation. We can listen to protestors and trust what they are saying. We can read what people like Albert J. Cleage, Jr. and Howard Thurman have written. We can let their experiences change us into people capable of assuming responsibility for our own thoughts and actions.

The Humanization of All People

Paulo Freire was a Brazilian educator and philosopher who died in 1997. His book, *Pedagogy of the Oppressed*, was first published in 1970 with a 50th Anniversary Edition published in 2018. Here are his recommendations for the humanization of all people.

Freire asserts that, in order to humanize all people, the domination of some by others must be overcome. The process starts with the oppressed, who must acquire critical thinking skills to understand how institutions of power work to deny them equality of treatment and justice. This will allow them to see what is a historical reality—a historical reality which can be transformed. Seeing institutions of power as a historical reality will prevent people of color from accepting and internalizing their oppression, which is what helps to destroy them.

Think about it: if society teaches you that whites are invulnerable and you accept that as truth, you will be impotent to change society. So how does a person of color, brainwashed into believing that whites are invulnerable, change this belief? Paulo Friere recommends dialogue—dialogue of revolutionary leaders with people of color. People of color bring their *empirical*, lived knowledge of reality to dialogue with revolutionary leaders. Revolutionary leaders bring their *critical* knowledge of reality to dialogue with people of color. Slowly the knowledge of those in dialogue becomes transformed into knowledge of the *causes* of reality. Once the causes are known, actions that will accomplish the human task—the transformation of reality in favor of the liberation of all people—can follow.

The process is not easy. Even when the oppression of some is resolved authentically, the focus must also move from the oppressed committing themselves to transformation to addressing how the humanity of the oppressors—which was lost in the exercise of oppression—can be restored. In other words, the goal is the liberation of all people.

Remember oneness consciousness! If one hurts, we all hurt. If one is oppressed, we all lose some of our humanity. The humanization of all people requires unity for liberation of all: unity among the oppressed, and unity of leaders with the oppressed.

Conclusion

Our current racial unrest is calling us to re-educate ourselves and heal our divisive world. It is calling us to oneness conscious where we see all persons and all our universe as good. We are all one.

May you have the courage to change and grow in love. And may we all grow and change in love together.

Acknowledgments

First and foremost I am grateful to the Universe for the time and freedom to enjoy this writing project. My understandings come from my experiences of living as a woman, mother, psychiatrist/psychoanalyst and practitioner of Christian contemplation.

All stories are true and are told with the permission of those involved. Where needed, in order to protect the confidentiality of those who have shared their experiences with me, I have changed their names and the identifying circumstances. I thank all who allowed me to tell their stories.

I have drawn illustrative examples from the literature. In instances where I may have misunderstood the authors cited, I apologize. I also apologize for those instances where the influence of others became so much a part of me that I may have overlooked acknowledging the source.

Betsy Diaz and Elaine Laity read the manuscript and gave me helpful guidance. Many, many thanks for your powerful input.

My everlasting gratitude goes to Cait Johnson for adding her spice of life to my words with her editorial expertise and her enthusiastic support of this project.

My additional thanks go to the entire team at Epigraph

Publishing Service for your support in the production of *Our Changing World: Understanding and Coping with It*.

I am also grateful to you, dear reader, for buying books and recommending them to your friends.

References

Ainsworth, M. D. S., Blehar, M. C., Waters, E., et al. (1978). *Patterns of attachment: A psychological study of the strange situation.* Hillsdale, NY: Lawrence Erlbaum.

Alexander, E. & Newell, K. (2017). *Living in a Mindful Universe: A Neurosurgeon's Journey into the Heart of Consciousness.* USA: Rodale.

Allman, J. M., Watson, K. K., Tetreault, N. A., et al. (2005). Intuition and autism: A possible role for Von Economo neurons. *TRENDS in Cognitive Sciences, 9*, 367-373.

Blakemore, S-J., & Decety, J. (2001). From the perception of action to the understanding of intention. *Nature Reviews Neuroscience, 2*, 561-567.

Bowlby, J. (1969). *Attachment.* New York: Basic Books.

Bowlby, J. (1973). *Separation.* New York: Basic Books.

Bowlby, J., (1988). *A secure base: Parent-child attachment and healthy human development.* New York: Basic Books.

Bourgeault, C. (2013). *The Holy Trinity and the Law of Three: Discovering the Radical Truth at the Heart of Christianity.* Boston: Shambhala Publications, Inc.

Brown, M. (2010). *The presence process: A journey into present moment *awareness*, Revised Edition. Vancouver, Canada: Namaste Publishing.

Bruteau, B. (2001). *The Grand Option: Personal Transformation and a New Creation*. Notre Dame, IN: University of Notre Dame Press.

Cannato, J. (2003). *Quantum Grace: Lenten Reflections on Creation and Connectedness*. Notre Dame, IN: Ave Maria Press.

Cannato, J. (2006). *Radical Amazement: Contemplative Lessons from Black Holes, Supernovas, and Other Wonders of the Universe*. Notre Dame, IN: Sorin Books.

Cannato, J. (2010). *Field of Compassion: How the New Cosmology is Transforming Spiritual Life*. Notre Dame, IN: Sorin Books.

Cone, J.H. (2011/2013). *The Cross and the Lynching Tree*. Maryknoll, NY: Orbis Books.

Cook-Greuter, S.R. (1999/2010). *Postautonomous Ego Development: A Study of Its Nature and Measurement*. Integral Publishers Dissertation Series.

Delio, I. (2013). *The Unbearable Wholeness of Being: God, Evolution, and the Power of Love*. Maryknoll, New York: Orbis Books.

Delio, I. (2016). Evolution toward personhood. In I. Delio (Ed.), *Personal transformation and a new creation: The spiritual revolution of Beatrice Bruteau* (pp. 109-134). Maryknoll, New York: Orbis Books.

de Zengotita, T. (2005/2007). *Mediated: How the Media Shape the World around You*. London: Bloomsbury Publishing.

di Pellegrino, G., Fadiga, L., Fogassi, L., et al. (1992). Understanding motor events: A neurophysiological study. *Experimental Brain Research, 91*, 176-180.

Gallese, V. (2001). The "shared manifold" hypothesis: From mirror neurons to empathy. *Journal of Consciousness Studies, 8*, 33-50.

Gallese, V. (2011). The two sides of mimesis: Mimetic theory, embodied simulation, and social identification. In S. R. Garrels (Ed.), *Mimesis and science: Empirical research on imitation and the mimetic theory of culture and religion* (pp. 87-108). East Lansing, MI: Michigan State University Press.

Gallese, V. & Sinigaglia, C. (2010). The bodily self as power for action. *Neuropsychologia, 48,* 746-755.

Gallese, V. Fadiga, L., Fogassi, L., et al. (1996). Action recognition in the premotor cortex. *Brain, 119,* 593-609.

Gallese, V., Fadiga, L., Fogassi, L. et al. (2002). Action representation and the inferior parietal lobule. In W. Prinz & B. Hommel (Eds.), *Attention and performance XIX: Common mechanisms in perception and action* (pp. 334-355). New York: Oxford University Press.

Garrison, A. & Severino, S.K. (2019). *Being Image: Simple Exercises to Claim Your Authentic Being,* Raleigh, North Carolina: Lulu Press, Inc.

Kalsched, D. (2013). *Trauma and the Soul: A Psycho-spiritual Approach to Human Development and Its Interruption.* New York, Routledge.

Kalsched, D. (2019). "Opening the Closed Heart: Affect Focused Clinical Work with the Victims of Early Trauma" Presentation at the IAAP Congress in Vienna, Austria: August 28.

Luke, H. M. (1987/2010). *Old age: Journey into simplicity.* Gt. Barrington, MA: Lindisfarne Books.

McGilchrist, I. (2009). *The Master and his Emissary; The Divided Brain and the Making of the Western World.* New Haven, CT: Yale University Press.

McKenna, J. (2010). *Spiritually Incorrect Enlightenment,* book two of *The Enlightenment Trilogy.* Wisefool Press.

McKenna, J. (2010). *Spiritual Warfare,* book three of *The Enlightenment Trilogy.* Wisefool Press.

Main, M. & Solomon, J. (1986). Discovery of an insecure-disorganized/disorientated attachment pattern. In T. B. Brazelton & M. Yogman (Eds.). *Affective development in infancy* (pp. 95-124). Norwood, NJ: Ablex.

Meltzoff, A. N. (2011). Out of the mouths of babes: Imitation, gaze and intentions in infant research—the "like me" framework. In S. R. Garrels (Ed.). *Mimesis and science: Empirical research on imitation and the mimetic theory of culture and religion* (pp. 55-74). East Lansing, MI: Michigan State University Press.

Mikulincer, M. & Shaver, P. R. (2010). *Attachment in adulthood: Structure, dynamics, and change.* New York: The Guilford Press.

Mukamel, R., Ekstrom, A. D., Kaplan J., et al. (2010). Single-neuron responses in humans during execution and observation of actions. *Current Biology, 20,* 750-756.

Palmer, P.J. (2000). *Let Your Life Speak: Listening for the Voice of Vocation.* San Francisco, CA: Jossey-Bass.

Palmer, P.J. (2011/2014). *Healing the Heart of Democracy: The Courage to Create a Politics Worthy of the Human Spirit.* San Francisco, CA: Jossey-Bass.

Panikkar, R. (2004). *Christophany: The Fullness of Man.* Maryknoll, NY: Orbis Books.

Porges, S.W. (2017). *The pocket guide to the polyvagal theory: The transformative power of feeling safe.* New York: W. W. Norton.

Primack, J.R., & Abrams, N.E. (2007). *The View from the Center of the Universe: Discovering Our Extraordinary Place in the Universe.* New York: Riverhead Books.

Rizzolatti, G., & Craighero, L. (2004). The mirror-neuron system. *Annual Review Neuroscience, 27,* 169-192.

Rizzolatti, G., Fadiga, L., Gallese, V., et al. (1996). Premotor cortex and the recognition of motor actions. *Cognitive Brain Research*, *3*, 131-141.

Roberts, B. (1993). *The Experience of No-Self: A Contemplative Journey*. Albany, NY: State University of New York Press.

Rohr, R. with Morrell, M. (2016). *The Divine Dance: The Trinity and Your Transformation*. New Kensington, PA: Whitaker House.

Shah, I. (1967). *Tales of the Dervishes: Teaching Stories of the Sufi Masters over the Past Thousand Years*. New York: Penguin Compass.

Shaia, A.J. (2006). *Beyond the Biography of Jesus: The Journey of Quadratos, Book 1*. Nashville, TN: Cold Tree Press.

Snyder, T. (2017). *On Tyranny: Twenty Lessons from the Twentieth Century*. New York: Tim Duggan Books.

Tolle, E. (2001). *Practising the Power of Now: A Guide to Spiritual Enlightenment*. London: Hodder & Stoughton, Ltd.

Tolle, W. (2003). *Stillness Speaks*. Novato, CA: New World Library.

Tolle, E. (1999/2004). *The Power of Now: A Guide to Spiritual Enlightenment*. Vancouver, B.C., Canada: Namaste Publishing.

Tolle, E. (2005/2016). *A New Earth: Awakening to Your Life's Purpose*. New York: Penguin Books.

Trevarthen, C. (2005). "Stepping away from the mirror: Pride and shame in adventures of companionship"—reflections on the nature and emotional needs of infant intersubjectivity. In C. S. Carter, L. Ahnert, K. E. Grossman, et al. (Eds.). *Attachment and bonding: A new synthesis* (pp. 55-84). Cambridge, MA: The MIT Press.

Zlatev, J., Racine, T.P., Sinha, C., et al. (2008). Intersubjectivity: What makes us human? In J. Zlatev, T. P. Racine, C. Sinha, et al. (Eds.), *The shared mind: Perspectives in intersubjectivity* (pp. 1-14). Philadelphia, PA: John Benjamins Publishing Company.

About the Author

Sally K. Severino M.D. earned her medical degree from Columbia University Roy and Diana Vagelos College of Physicians and Surgeons. She served seventeen years at New York-Presbyterian Hospital/Westchester Division before becoming Professor and Executive Vice-Chair, Department of Psychiatry, University of New Mexico Health Sciences Center, where she is currently Professor Emeritus of Psychiatry. Certified by the American Psychoanalytic Association, she served as the first woman president of the American College of Psychoanalysts. She is grounded in the Christian contemplative tradition, which she has practiced some twenty-five years. She lives in Rio Rancho, New Mexico.

www.ingramcontent.com/pod-product-compliance
Lightning Source LLC
LaVergne TN
LVHW011427080426
835512LV00005B/312